EMPIRE STATE BUILDING

Erinn Banting and Heather Kissock

www.av2books.com

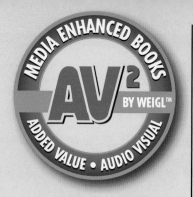

AV² provides enriched content that supplements and complements this book Weigl's AV² books strive to create inspired learning and engage young minds in a total learning experience.

Your AV² Media Enhanced books come alive with...

Audio
Listen to sections of the book read aloud.

Key Words
Study vocabulary, and complete a matching word activity.

Video
Watch informative video clips.

Quizzes
Test your knowledge.

Embedded Weblinks
Gain additional information for research.

Slide Show
View images and captions, and prepare a presentation.

Go to **www.av2books.com**, and enter this book's unique code.

BOOK CODE

X792088

AV² by Weigl brings you media enhanced books that support active learning.

Try This!
Complete activities and hands-on experiments.

... and much, much more!

Published by AV² by Weigl
350 5th Avenue, 59th Floor
New York, NY 10118

Website: www.av2books.com   www.weigl.com

Library of Congress Cataloging-in-Publication Data
Banting, Erinn.
  Empire State Building / Erinn Banting.
     p. cm. -- (Virtual field trip)
  Summary: "Explores the history, the people, and the science behind the construction of the Empire State Building-- Provided by publisher.
  Includes index.
  ISBN 978-1-62127-462-9 (hardcover : alk. paper) -- ISBN 978-1-62127-468-1 (softcover : alk. paper)
  1. Empire State Building (New York, N.Y.)--Juvenile literature. 2. New York (N.Y.)--Buildings, structures, etc.--Juvenile literature. I. Title.
  F128.8.E46B36 2014
  974.7'1--dc23

                    2012044672

Printed in the United States of America in North Mankato, Minnesota
1 2 3 4 5 6 7 8 9 0 17 16 15 14 13

032013
WEP301112

Editor: Heather Kissock
Design: Terry Paulhus

Every reasonable effort has been made to trace ownership and to obtain permission to reprint copyright material. The publishers would be pleased to have any errors or omissions brought to their attention so that they may be corrected in subsequent printings.

Weigl acknowledges Getty Images as its primary image supplier for this title.

Contents

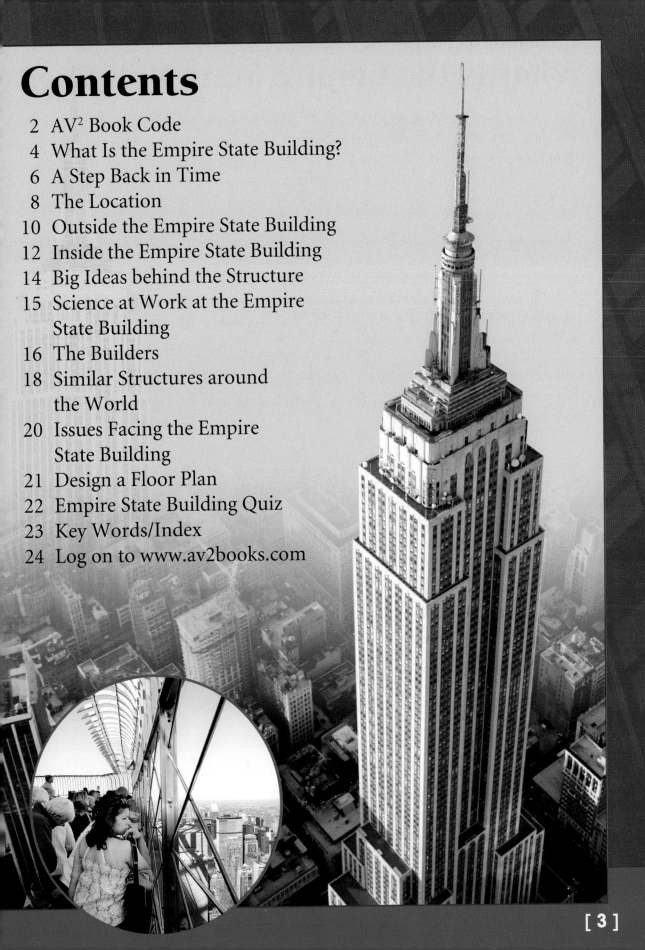

2 AV² Book Code

4 What Is the Empire State Building?

6 A Step Back in Time

8 The Location

10 Outside the Empire State Building

12 Inside the Empire State Building

14 Big Ideas behind the Structure

15 Science at Work at the Empire State Building

16 The Builders

18 Similar Structures around the World

20 Issues Facing the Empire State Building

21 Design a Floor Plan

22 Empire State Building Quiz

23 Key Words/Index

24 Log on to www.av2books.com

What Is the Empire State Building?

The Empire State Building in New York City is one of the world's most visited buildings. The tall office building was built in 1931, during a period known as the **Great Depression**. At this time, many people struggled to find jobs. The **investors** who funded the construction of the Empire State Building gave work to thousands of people in need.

During its construction, the Empire State Building set a world record as the world's tallest structure. Builders used an **assembly line** method for constructing the tower. This forever changed the way people raised buildings. Materials were pre-assembled off site to save time, builders worked in shifts around the clock, and construction took place on different levels of the building at the same time. The 102-story tower took only one year and 45 days to build.

Today, the New York City skyline would be hard to imagine without its skyscrapers. They serve as a reminder of the history, growth, and prosperity of one of the largest cities in the United States.

In the early 1900s, New York was the center for industry, business, and culture. As a result, the state was given the nickname "The Empire State." This is how the building received its name.

Snapshot of New York State

New York State is located in the northeastern part of the United States. It shares its southern border with New Jersey and Pennsylvania and its northern border with the Canadian provinces of Ontario and Quebec. Connecticut, Massachusetts, and Vermont lie to its east.

INTRODUCING NEW YORK

CAPITAL CITY: Albany

FLAG:

MOTTO: *Excelsior* (Ever Upward)

NICKNAME: The Empire State

POPULATION: 19,465,197 (2011)

ADMITTED TO THE UNION: July 26, 1788

CLIMATE: Warm and humid summers with cold winters

SUMMER TEMPERATURE: Average of 82° Fahrenheit (28° Celsius)

WINTER TEMPERATURE: Average of −7°F (−22°C)

TIME ZONE: Eastern Standard Time (EST)

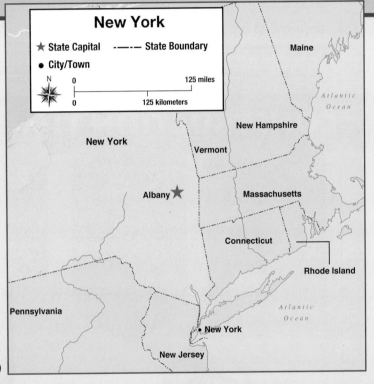

New York

★ State Capital   ----- State Boundary
● City/Town

N   0   125 miles
     0   125 kilometers

Maine
Atlantic Ocean
New Hampshire
New York
Vermont
Albany ★
Massachusetts
Connecticut
Rhode Island
Pennsylvania
Atlantic Ocean
● New York
New Jersey

New York Symbols

New York has several official symbols. Some symbols represent the features that distinguish the area from other parts of the United States. Others indicate the unique place New York has in the history of the country.

OFFICIAL FLOWER
Rose

OFFICIAL BIRD
Eastern Bluebird

OFFICIAL TREE
Sugar Maple

A Step Back in Time

In the 1900s, cities in the United States boomed. **Architects** and industry leaders wanted to build structures that represented the wealth and success of their companies. Towers grew taller, larger, and more elaborate. In cities such as New York, architects competed to see whose tower could reach the highest.

In 1929, a businessman named John Jakob Raskob decided he wanted to build the world's tallest structure. After securing investors, he hired an architecture firm called Shreve, Lamb & Harmon Associates to design the building. A company called Starrett Brothers and Eken was hired to actually build the tower.

CONSTRUCTION TIMELINE

1929
John Jakob Raskob and a group of investors form Empire State, Inc. and decide to build the world's tallest structure.

1929
The Waldorf Astoria is demolished to make room for the new office building.

1930
Excavation of the site where the building now stands begins on January 22.

1930
Construction of the Empire State Building starts on March 17.

The Waldorf Astoria Hotel was one of New York's elite hotels. It opened in 1893.

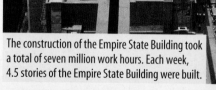

The construction of the Empire State Building took a total of seven million work hours. Each week, 4.5 stories of the Empire State Building were built.

Building the tallest structure in the world took much planning and work. The building not only had to be the tallest, it also had to be safe, attractive, and built in a very short period. The Empire State Building was raised at record speed. Nearly one story was built each day. A crew of more than 3,400 workers worked seven days a week for nearly a year. Construction was completed in 1931.

Construction of the Empire State Building took only 16 months.

1930
The Empire State Building is declared the world's tallest building.

1931
The Empire State Building officially opens.

1972
The Empire State Building loses its title as "world's tallest building" with the construction of the World Trade Center towers, also in New York City.

1986
The Empire State Building is declared a National Historic Landmark by the U.S. government.

The Empire State Building was named the world's tallest building before its construction was completed.

Buildings are given National Historic Landmark status to acknowledge their importance to the country as a whole.

The Location

The Empire State Building is located in the heart of Manhattan, an island in New York City. Manhattan was and is the city's key business district. The Empire State Building was built to be an office building and today is home to approximately 1,000 businesses.

The building was constructed on the site of the original Waldorf Astoria Hotel. The owners of the hotel decided to sell the property when the real estate prices in the area rose. They felt they could make a profit on the land and build a new hotel in another part of town. Raskob and his associates bought the property for about $20 million. The hotel was then demolished to make room for the new skyscraper.

Even though the Empire State Building is now surrounded by newer, more modern buildings, it remains an important part of the New York skyline.

The Empire State Building Today

The Empire State Building has always been more than an office building. Even though it is no longer the world's tallest building, it remains a landmark for the city of New York. Each year, the building attracts more about 4 million visitors, who ride the elevators to the upper floors and take in the view of the surrounding city.

Weight The building weighs 365,000 tons (331,000 tonnes).

Height The structure is 1,454 feet (443 metres) tall to the top of the lightning rod. The antenna **spire** is 204 feet (62 m) high.

Area East to west, the building is 424 feet (129 m). North to south, the building is 187 feet (57 m).

Outside the Empire State Building

*The Empire State Building was designed in the art deco style that was popular at the time. This style of building features **geometric** patterns, strong colors, and angular curves.*

Facade The facade, or face, of the Empire State Building is made from limestone that has been arranged in a series of vertical bands. In between the bands are the building's steel-framed windows. **Setbacks** were incorporated into the building's design. These allow the building to taper inward as it rises from the ground.

The Empire State Building has more than 6,500 windows.

Tourists must enter the Empire State Building through the Fifth Avenue entrance. The other entrances are for people conducting business in the building.

Entrances People can enter the Empire State Building through five entrance points. The main entrance is located on Fifth Avenue, one of New York's main thoroughfares. Three-story tall windows run above the entrance. These windows are enclosed within two columns. Each column is topped with a sculpture of an eagle. The words "Empire State" are set between the two eagles.

Outdoor Observation Deck The outdoor observation deck is located on the 86th floor. From here, visitors can take in a 360-degree view of the city. For those wanting a closer look, high-powered binoculars are mounted near the edge of the deck. The entire deck is surrounded by mesh wiring to ensure the safety of the building's visitors.

On a clear day, visitors to the Empire State Building can see a view that extends 80 miles (129 kilometers).

Lighting At night, the top of the Empire State Building is lit up. Colored lights are used to represent different occasions. For example, on Valentine's Day, the lights are red, white, and pink. On Earth Day, they are green.

On Memorial Day, the Empire State Building features red, white, and blue lighting.

Spire The spire forms the pointed top of the building. It was originally meant to serve as a docking area for **dirigibles**, but safety issues quickly cancelled these plans. The spire is capped by a lightning rod that protects the building during thunderstorms. Several broadcasting antennas are also located on the spire.

All of New York City's major FM radio and television stations send their broadcasting signals from the antennas at the top of the Empire State Building.

VIRTUAL TOUR

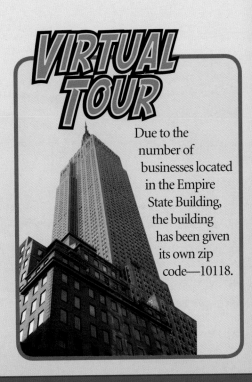

Due to the number of businesses located in the Empire State Building, the building has been given its own zip code—10118.

Inside the Empire State Building

The interior of the Empire State Building follows the art deco theme of the exterior, with decorative and colorful elements found throughout the building. While much of the building remains office space, several areas have been developed specifically for visitors to the city.

Lobby Art deco stylings are the centerpiece of the Empire State Building's lobby. A mural painted with gold leaf covers the lobby ceiling. Panels of **cast** glass adorn the corridors and elevator banks. Ornate chandeliers greet people entering the lobby through the 34th and 35th Street entrances. Sheets of marble decorate the lobby's walls and floors.

A mural of the Empire State Building sits behind the lobby reception desk.

The Empire State Building's elevators move 1,400 feet (426 m) per second. The elevator ride from the lobby to the 86th floor takes less than one minute.

Elevators The Empire State Building has 73 elevators, including several service elevators. The elevators do not travel to all floors. Instead, different groupings have been set up to service specific floors. One set of elevators, for instance, services floors three through seven. Another services floors seven through eighteen. This system allows people to get to their floors more quickly than if every elevator were to stop at every floor.

Observatory The observatory is located on the 102nd floor, 16 stories higher than the observation decks. The observatory is completely glass-enclosed and is much smaller than the lower observation decks, but it provides visitors with an exceptional view of New York City and its surrounding area.

The observatory is the highest point open to the public in New York City.

Like the outdoor observation deck, the indoor deck also offers visitors a spectacular view of New York City and its surrounding area.

Indoor Observation Deck Besides its outdoor observation deck, the 86th floor features an indoor observation deck as well. The indoor deck is fully enclosed, with windows all around. It provides people with a view of the city while protecting them from wet or chilly weather.

The Skyride features an 18-foot (5.5-m) high-definition movie screen.

Skyride Visitors can experience a flight through New York City when they visit the Skyride. Located on the Empire State Building's second floor, the Skyride is a virtual tour simulator. A 30-minute movie takes the audience on a tour of the city. Their seats are positioned on a platform that moves in tandem with events unfolding on the movie screen.

Big Ideas behind the Structure

The designers and builders who created the Empire State building had to have a firm understanding of science to build the world's largest structure. They had to know the correct materials to use and how to put the building together in a way that guaranteed stability and strength.

Steel columns and beams form a three-dimensional grid in the structure of the building.

Loads

Designers and architects must take **loads** into consideration when building a tower, such as the Empire State Building. There are different kinds of loads that architects have to consider before construction begins. The weight of the building, including all the materials needed to build it, is called the dead load. Weight from items such as furniture and people is called the live load. The kind of soil where the building is constructed also affects loads. Soil can sometimes shift or move after construction is complete. The degree to which a building shifts is called the settlement load. Wind loads are also important to consider, especially in the construction of high buildings. The force of the wind blowing against a structure impacts how it is constructed.

Tension and Compression

To make a building that will survive the forces of nature, architects must consider the forces of **tension** and **compression**. Tension pulls materials apart, while compression pushes materials together. Wind loads create both compression and tension. The side of the building that is being blown against is acted upon by tension, while the opposite side is acted upon by compression. The designers used steel to construct the Empire State Building because it resists compression. Each steel beam was fastened on all sides, including the top and bottom. This resulted in each cube in the frame having a limited range of movement.

Even in winds up to 110 miles (177 km) per hour, the Empire State Building only moves 1.48 inches (3.76 centimeters).

Science at Work at the Empire State Building

Constructing the tallest structure in the world took planning, labor, and the latest technology. The people who worked on the Empire State Building used tools, materials, and methods that operate under basic principles of science.

Pulleys used on the cranes helped lower steel beams into place.

Pulleys

Large cranes were used to lift heavy steel beams up to each floor and to put the beams in place. Cranes use pulleys to move heavy objects. A pulley changes the direction of the force, making it easier to lift things. Pulleys consist of wheels wrapped in rope or wire. On one end of the rope is a hook that attaches to the object that needs to be lifted. On the other end, a person pulls the rope. The pulley uses a wheel to help distribute the weight, making it feel lighter so it can be moved.

Steam Engines

Enormous shovels were used to dig the giant pit where the **foundation** was built. These machines were powered by steam engines. Invented in the 1700s, steam engines were used in factories, vehicles, and machinery. The operation of the engines relied on a system that used water and **pistons**. Water was heated in large boilers, which created steam. The steam

Using steam shovels helped get the foundation dug in only two months.

expanded and compressed in the engine. The compressed steam moved a piece called a piston. The movement of the piston was connected to the moving parts of the engine, which forced the engines to go. Using steam-powered shovels saved a great deal of time and helped move along the construction of the Empire State Building.

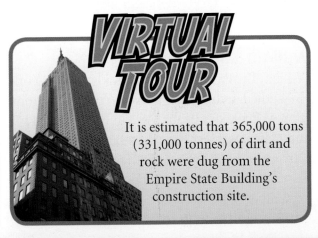

VIRTUAL TOUR

It is estimated that 365,000 tons (331,000 tonnes) of dirt and rock were dug from the Empire State Building's construction site.

The Builders

The investors, architects, and designers who had the vision to build the Empire State Building were important to its creation. Without the workers who helped build it, however, the building would have remained a blueprint.

Construction on the New York Public Library began in 1897. The work was completed in 1911.

Arthur Loomis Harmon

Designer

Arthur Loomis Harmon was born in Chicago, Illinois, in 1878. Harmon

The Trump Building is also known as 40 Wall Street. This is the building's New York address.

studied at the Art Institute of Chicago and at Columbia University. He graduated in 1901 and went on to work at many New York-based architecture firms. In 1929, he joined Shreve & Lamb. As head designer, Harmon had to rely on an expert and skilled contracting company. He hired Starrett Brothers and Eken, an experienced contracting firm in New York City. They had worked on many other buildings, including 40 Wall Street, which is now known as The Trump Building.

Richmond Harold Shreve Architect

Shreve, Lamb & Harmon Associates was founded in 1929 by Richmond Harold Shreve, William Lamb, and Arthur Loomis Harmon. Shreve was born in the Canadian province of Nova Scotia in 1877 and studied architecture at Cornell University in New York. After graduating in 1902, he taught at the university for four years before joining the firm of Carrère and Hastings. The firm was one of the most successful in New York City and was known for its design of important buildings, such as the New York Public Library.

William Lamb Architect

William Lamb was born in Brooklyn, New York, in 1883. He studied architecture at New York's Columbia University, and later, at École des Beaux-Arts in Paris. In 1911, he joined Carrère and Hastings. Over time, Lamb and Shreve became partners in Carrère and Hastings. Together, they worked on many of the firm's projects, including the Standard Oil Building, an early skyscraper completed in 1922. In 1924, Shreve and Lamb left Carrère and Hastings to create their own firm.

The Standard Oil Building was designated a New York City landmark in 1995. It is known for its pyramid tower and its curved façade.

Steelworkers

Steel is much stronger than iron, and it is used in many structures, including the Empire State Building. Steelworkers manufacture steel. Steel is made by refining iron. Refined iron is heated so that impurities, such as carbon, are removed. Large amounts of oxygen are blasted through powerful furnaces. The oxygen combines with the carbon in the iron.

Steelworkers shaped the beams used in the construction of the Empire State Building.

Lifting Crews

Lifting crews ensured that building materials reached workers at various levels of the structure.

Lifting crews used cranes to move the heavy steel beams. The men that made up these crews were called derrick operators. A derrick is a type of large crane that is used to lift, move, and place heavy objects. A derrick operator uses levers and pedals to move the boom, which is the long rod at the top of the crane. During construction of the Empire State Building, derricks were used to hoist and place enormous steel beams.

Riveting Teams

Riveting teams put **rivets** in place. Each riveting team included a "heater," a "catcher," a "bucker-up," and a "gunman." The heater put the rivets in a **forge** until they were red hot. Tongs were then used to throw the rivets up to the catcher, who waited on the floors above. Catchers used old tins to catch the fiery rivets. Once they caught a rivet, they would pick it up with another set of tongs and put it through the holes of the beams that needed to be fastened. The bucker-up held the rivet steady so the gunman could hammer it into place with a special riveting hammer.

For safety purposes, it was important for riveting teams to work cooperatively.

Similar Structures around the World

The race to build the world's tallest structure did not end when the Empire State Building took the title in 1931. Many other architects continued to look for ways to surpass the building's 102 stories. Today, the world has many structures that exceed the height of the Empire State Building.

Willis Tower

BUILT: 1973
LOCATION: Chicago, United States
DESIGN: Bruce Graham
DESCRIPTION: Plans for the Willis Tower, formerly known as the Sears Tower, began in 1969. At the time, Sears Roebuck & Co. operated one of the largest chains of department stores in the United States. The company built the tower for its 350,000 employees. The 1,450-foot (442-m) tall building has more office space than any tower in the United States.

Willis Tower is currently the tallest building in the western hemisphere.

The Petronas Towers have a skybridge connecting the two towers. People can walk from one building to the other on a glass-enclosed bridge 558 feet (170 m) above the ground.

Petronas Towers

BUILT: 1998
LOCATION: Kuala Lumpur, Malaysia
DESIGN: César Pelli
DESCRIPTION: Both of the Petronas Towers rise to a height of 1,483 feet (452 m). The design of the towers was inspired by the art of a religion called Islam. Although they look identical, the two towers were built by two different construction companies. The companies competed to see who could raise their tower the fastest.

Jin Mao Tower

BUILT: 1998
LOCATION: Shanghai, China
DESIGN: Skidmore, Owings & Merrill
DESCRIPTION: The design of the Jin Mao Tower was inspired by Chinese architecture. The octagon-shaped building tapers as it stretches into the sky. Due to its location, the tower was built with special reinforcements to protect it from collapse in extreme weather or during earthquakes.

The Jin Mao Tower is 88 stories high. It features office buildings, a hotel, and an observation deck.

Taipei 101

BUILT: 2004
LOCATION: Taipei, Taiwan
DESIGN: C.Y. Lee and Partners
DESCRIPTION: At 1,670 feet (509 m), Taipei 101 is currently the third tallest building in the world. The building, which resembles a stick of bamboo, was built based on the number eight. Each of the eight sections of the building has eight floors. The number eight is considered lucky by many Chinese people.

Taipei 101 was also designed to look like a pagoda. This is a type of religious building found in various parts of Asia.

Issues Facing the Empire State Building

Constructing a tower as large as the Empire State Building had a significant effect on New York City. It changed the face of the New York skyline and impacted the city and the people who lived there. Over the years, the building has faced several challenges. The city has taken steps to preserve this important landmark.

WHAT WAS THE ISSUE?

Wind, humidity, and **acid rain** were damaging the exterior of the building.	The building was not built to be energy efficient.

EFFECTS

Parts of the building's facade were **corroded** due to **weathering**.	Heat and air were escaping from the building causing more heat to be required to warm the building.

ACTION TAKEN

The damaged areas were repaired or replaced. In 2009, the facade was waterproofed to protect it from rain damage.	As part of a restoration program announced in 2009, the building's windows have been refurbished to provide better insulation.

Design a Floor Plan

Architects and designers use blueprints to plan their buildings. Blueprints include overall images of the size and shape of the building, as well as the interior of the building. Floor plans show each of the rooms on each floor of a building. Using a few simple tools, design a floor plan.

Materials
- graph paper
- a ruler
- a pencil
- an eraser
- a blue or black marker

Instructions

1. First, decide which kind of building you would like to design. It could be a house, an apartment block, a school, an office building, or a shopping center. Then, make a list of all the rooms that will be inside the building.

2. Start by designing the main room on the first floor. Decide where it should be located, how big it should be, and how it will connect to other rooms. Each square on the graph paper is equal to one square foot (0.1 sq. m) in a room.

3. Using a ruler and a pencil, trace the outline of the room. Add doors and windows using the special symbols that architects use. These symbols can be viewed at www.stanfordartedventures.com/create/try_this_floorplan.htm.

4. Draw the remaining rooms. Make sure they connect to one another. Look at how many entrances and exits are needed. Does the building need bathrooms or a kitchen? Think about whether your building needs stairs or an elevator up to the next floor. Add these things to your floor plan.

5. Once the floor plan is complete, trace over the pencil lines with marker. Now, the blueprint is complete.

Empire State Building Quiz

Q How long did the construction of the Empire State Building take?

A 1 year and 45 days

Q What was the name of the architectural firm that designed the Empire State Building?

A Shreve, Lamb & Harmon

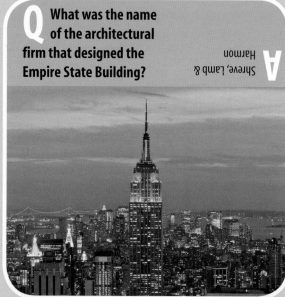

Q What is a load?

A A load is a force that impacts how a structure must be built.

Q What was the role of a gunman on a riveting team?

A The gunman hammered the rivet into place with a special riveting hammer.

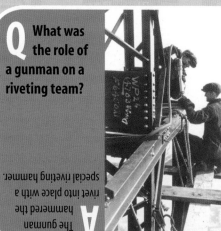

Key Words

acid rain: precipitation containing pollution that can harm the environment

architects: people who design and supervise the construction of buildings

assembly line: a sequence of machines, tools, workers, and operations in a factory, arranged so that at each stage a further process is carried out

cast: formed into a particular shape by pouring into a mold

compression: the act of being flattened or squeezed together by pressure

corroded: eaten or worn away

dirigibles: types of airships sometimes called blimps

forge: a furnace where metals are heated

foundation: the part of a building that helps support its weight

geometric: pertaining to a type of mathematics that deals with the relationships between points, lines, and angles

Great Depression: a period during the 1930s when many people lost their jobs

investors: people who support a project with money

loads: weights or sources of pressure carried by an object

pistons: discs that slide back and forth in a hollow cylinder

rivets: metal items which are used to fasten large pieces of metal together

setbacks: steplike recessions in the rise of a tall building

spire: a tapering structure at the top of a building

tension: the state of being stretched

weathering: the breaking down of stone by the action of rain, snow, etc.

Index

Art Deco 10, 12

compression 14

Great Depression 4

iron 17

Jin Mao Tower 19

loads 14, 22

Petronas Towers 18
pulleys 15

Raskob, John Jakob 6, 8
restoration 20

Shreve, Lamb and Harmon 6, 16, 22
steam engines 15
steel 10, 14, 15, 17

Taipei 101 19
tension 14

Waldorf Astoria Hotel 6, 8
Willis Tower 18

Log on to www.av2books.com

AV² by Weigl brings you media enhanced books that support active learning. Go to www.av2books.com, and enter the special code found on page 2 of this book. You will gain access to enriched and enhanced content that supplements and complements this book. Content includes video, audio, weblinks, quizzes, a slide show, and activities.

AV² Online Navigation

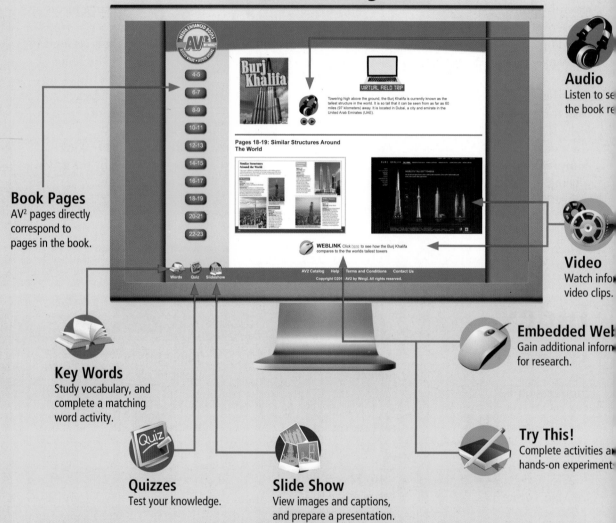

Audio
Listen to se
the book re

Video
Watch info
video clips.

Embedded Web
Gain additional inform
for research.

Try This!
Complete activities a
hands-on experiment

Book Pages
AV² pages directly correspond to pages in the book.

Key Words
Study vocabulary, and complete a matching word activity.

Quizzes
Test your knowledge.

Slide Show
View images and captions, and prepare a presentation.

AV² was built to bridge the gap between print and digital. We encourage you to tell us what you like and what you want to see in the future.

Sign up to be an AV² Ambassador at www.av2books.com/ambassador.